PLENITUDE

POEMS

Daniel
Sarah
Karasik

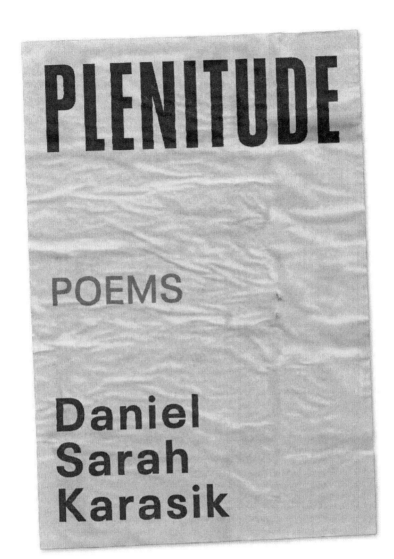

PLENITUDE

POEMS

Daniel Sarah Karasik

Book*hug Press
Toronto 2022

Library and Archives Canada Cataloguing in Publication

Title: Plenitude / Daniel Sarah Karasik.

Names: Karasik, Daniel, 1986- author.

Description: Poems.

Identifiers: Canadiana (print) 2021037585X | Canadiana (ebook) 20210375868

ISBN 9781771667357 (softcover)

ISBN 9781771667364 (EPUB)

ISBN 9781771667371 (PDF)

Classification: LCC PS8621.A6224 P54 2022 | DDC C811/.6—dc23

The production of this book was made possible through the generous assistance of the Canada Council for the Arts and the Ontario Arts Council. Book*hug Press also acknowledges the support of the Government of Canada through the Canada Book Fund and the Government of Ontario through the Ontario Book Publishing Tax Credit and the Ontario Book Fund.

Book*hug Press acknowledges that the land on which we operate is the traditional territory of many nations, including the Mississaugas of the Credit, the Anishnabeg, the Chippewa, the Haudenosaunee, and the Wendat peoples. We recognize the enduring presence of many diverse First Nations, Inuit, and Métis peoples and are grateful for the opportunity to meet, work, and learn on this territory.

Book*hug Press

For my comrades.

CONTENTS

4

5

6

messianic time

imagine there were no oppression to shape our identities. instead: limitless forms of descriptive difference not essentialized and politicized by violence. if we were to say *I* in such a world, we might mean almost nothing but a historied, futured, networked locus of desire

radiant incipience

and if some came to say trans rights
and others came out since they thought
it'd be a big old party,
celebration of fuck the police,
a moment when the rules
might be suspended,
that's all good. I mean,
the contradictions
of mass gatherings
interest me, it's not
that I'm incurious,
but that I find those motives
are all one.

when the police locked comrades
in the library and lied
about it, our chant said
trans rights are human rights,
but what we meant was
rights won't save us
if we don't protect each other.

a comrade said
the read-in of trans authors was
the happiest she'd ever been
at any protest except
possibly a kiss-in once.

the revolution will need savvy
party planners, capable
of seeing
how the carnival's already here.

a radiant incipience.
just waiting to be generalized.

energy

calling riots
counterproductive
is like calling a tornado
unstrategic. build a wind turbine
or get out of the way

stages of grief

1.

in which
you believe
any and all
disclosure
of your pain
is a step
towards healing it

2.

in which
you recognize
the political mechanisms
that encourage us to mistake
disclosure for healing
while depriving us
of resources
for transforming
one into the other

3.

in which
you perceive
the dominant system's
foundational assumption
that healing is impossible
but aspirations to it
infinitely monetizable,
that system's
clear material interest
in replicating harm
as it pretends
to facilitate
repair

make/work

firms and states proliferate
the logics that say: work
will set you free! when we
deliberate upon this flimsy
sales pitch long enough, we see
the freedom offered is, though spectral,
sometimes faintly legible
in sudden brief intensities,
those slipstreamed moments
of transcendence
that break the clock's count.

what's the work, or which the ways
that work can escape clockwork?

is it dangerous to sing of freedom
in the unfree work? at risk of serving
bosses, volunteering propaganda
for those who command?

or is it to refuse sentimentalities
of difficulty *and* of ease,
to insist that all making's pain
but fuck pain that's unchosen,
to say: we'll be free or freer only
when empowered to elect
the suffering
we find most pleasing—
useful
or voluptuous

Against the Law

Because the law, I hear, is a technology
of power, I frenzy on a Sunday night
in search of wooden pencils
needed for the LSAT.
Blow the test, or feel I do,
and mind and hardly mind, because
the law, I hear, is a machine
of capital, or let's not be
quite so reductive, let's just say
the law gives text to power
built elsewhere, in boardrooms
or in the streets, is male
in its forms of enactment, phallic
in its sophistries, its stern Socratic certainties
about the weight of argument
in settling or discerning right.
I took some pretty selfies in tight panties
last night that my lover, pegging me
as lithe enough to slide
into them nicely, bought me
prior to my masculine evaluation date.
How wet and hard I would have been
if I had worn them on that morning,
lace beyond the proctor's gaze, infringement
of unwritten rules from law's halcyon phase
when it was plausible enough, for some,
to think the law respectable, as instrument
or way to spend one's days. My teacher who
had lawyer brothers called the law a form
of trash collection, cleanup crews invoked
when the ripe mess grew just unbearable.
Pleasure, healing not the guiding principles.
Despite what I thought at age eight, not a clear way
to make an ache for justice wearable, as if

a sterling silver pin on a lapel. Believe me,
I'd prevaricate like this upon just about
any work it fell to me to do. But standing
against law, against the law, against it
like a thief who steals bread for some hungry strangers
whom she'll never meet is stood against the law
that stands against the whole of us,
that lays waste to, denies so many
possibilities in us—well, that just seems
a simple, mandatory way
to advocate for you.

scratch

shout-out to anyone who dotes daily on the newer trauma because
that means the older trauma can stay buried, irradiating the
neighbourhood, though sometimes when you walk the new trauma
it drags you to the old burial place & scratches & claws & scratches
at the ground, almost helping you make a connection you almost
make

Among Other White Jews

The blue refuge
of melancholic caught-between.
I don't know how
to reconcile my guilt at having
this much power
with rage at having so much less
than is imputed to me
by those who would like to see me dead.
Not safety, clearly. And no use to anyone
but those who'd like to see us...if not dead,
then at least stuck, quiescent: willing
to accept the bargain
whiteness and its empires offer us.

Amid the dust of police precincts
rubbled, mulched, in streets where tear gas
seeps through broken windows (sleepless
millions pressed against them,
the 12-megapixel cameras
in their history-documenting
sex toys filming), nameless friends
invite us to stand with them
in their work and pain and even fun,
array our forces on their side.
Or, sure, we could just hide, and wait
for whiteness to evict us. Like it's always done.

silences

poetry about silence wins prizes
as long as it's silent about Palestine.
irony is a poetic device
that lets you not say what you mean
too loudly. what's done
to Palestine is done in my name.
my name is a prosaic device
for denying what's unnameable.
how can you
not think
of concentration camps
at the sight of that vicious
infrastructure
I asked an elder of my tribe
when I was 19
and had just passed easily
through Qalandia Checkpoint.
how can you not think
of concentration camps
she asked me in turn.
how can you not see
that the price of this
false calm
is paid by others.
how can you not see the price.
what we pay, too,
and what we can't. all the debts
that won't be settled. forgiveness
no one living
has the power
to offer.

Regarding the Prophetic Tradition

It takes a certain hubris to extrapolate that way.
It takes a certain faith.
A Jewish predilection for the vatic voice, you might say.
A sentimental mode, maybe.
The wish not just to see truth and to say it,
but to be moved by it, and to move.
The poets have described the world;
the point, however, is
                              to change
yourself into the kind of person
who can suss out where the most
effective point of struggle is
and go there, or support those
who are there already, on life's side.
And to get free. Which is to say,
to sing desire into a loving,
fighting sociality.

trans-socialist

as in a public that would be safe and good for trans people.

as in what is safe and good for trans people producing a public more adequate, more worthy of the name.

as in a socialism whose real movement moves beyond itself.

as in communism (but why not just say that).

as in a communism that would abolish debates over when and how to say "communism."

as in a communism that would abolish every poem that is a poem against the police because obviously no police.

as in the condition in which gender is transformed because it's no longer mobilized to serve institutions of social domination.

as in the condition in which gender is reborn as pure play.

as in the state of affairs in which the state is a memory recalled only upon consulting the archives.

as in a warm hearth held in common but also there's privacy.

as in erotic community but soundproofed bedrooms.

as in cocks in cute skirts as in cunts that are cocks as in t4t4t4t4t...

as in strife and envy and competition and violence yes sometimes ineluctably violence but outside the death cult of capital, of the wage.

as in no bosses no cops no shortcuts no utopia no final peace no (in the final analysis) final poem against the police.

as in beyond the last snow-capped summit, another

as in the prophecy that says there may be no last prophecy but this can't be it, keep struggling

as in the wish that says there may be no last wish but this isn't it,
keep going

Plenitude

If, in my one body, I'd a cock & pussy both,
I wouldn't use them arbitrarily, toggling
back and forth on whims. Instead I'd make
a calendar: my cock today,
the *lendemain* my pussy.

> *Not unlike,*
you'll say, *how you flop from your cock*
to your bumhole as the prime site
where your desire inheres—and now
you need a pussy too? Be satisfied
with what your butt can do.
Dysphoria, you'll say, *okay,*
but that's subjective, commonplace
fluidity, confusion
that you feel sometimes; c'mon, admit
that craving to appropriate
a pussy (given all you have,
all your enormous privilege) is, frankly,
entitled—acquisitive.

I say: do you believe these things
are zero-sum? Like, when I claim dissatisfaction
with my cock alone, and voice a wish
to have a cunt also—do you think
this requires someone else lose their own?
As if the global store of cunts
were finite?

Ugh
You're just a man you're playing games you're co-opting you're not a
real—

    I've seen you in the patriarchy
      Saw you at that club one night
        The Patriarchy
      Nice tunes there
    Did you see him
      I saw him he was there
        And now he wants to be a she? a they—?
Ha ha ha
    Ha ha
      HA!
        HA HA!
Guys maybe we don't need to laugh
        HA HA—!

But I make few claims of membership.
I have no narrative to offer
where from childhood I felt sure
I was a girl. To measure by the company
in which I felt at home, more likely I
believed I was a book. I know I felt
weak and enjoyed that, fetishized
my softness, vulnerability
before I knew them to be
"coded female." But that's still
not the thing.

The thing, my claim,
the whole of it, is just: I'd love to have
a cock and pussy. Interchangeable
to suit the day. And also would like Gender
to be overthrown, and every woman
now alive and also every boi
to adore me—goals
that need not be contradictory.

I don't ask much.
I blink, demure.
Solicitously, I extend
my round bottom to you.

hustle

a roll of dice in earshot of the sea,
some kind of game, vacationers at play.
it seems as if my hair is longer
than the locks of any other
cock-possessing hustler here.
my wool coat's cut
confuses locals: femme
or dandy? does the latter concept
scan around this place? perhaps they just
say *gay*. so many of our friends,
even, on some level believe
we're hustling: trans fems want
attention, access—that old phobic
line. I do
want those things, honestly,
if often as necessities
for staying afloat: cis systems
(grim economies)
crush us when we lack access,
spurn attention. I do get so bored
of us, of me, sometimes.
and I also love us, myself,
sometimes, too. in places
like this seaside town, off season,
Grindr showing just a dozen locals,
it's not hard to feel my femme-cut coat's
a pose, albeit a convincing one (brief Panic!
at the railway bathroom: *excuse me!*
I think a lady went in there!),
the whole thing just a fad like bigots say,
not capturing real differences
in gender, genre, species, kind,
just style. exteriorities.

but then I look at men.
and it's like.
oh.

Tóngzhì

Xi, chairman and president of the Chinese People's Republic, wants
to bring back the word *comrade*, jingoistically. But now he's stymied
by the way the kids have spun that word: delightfully,

to name a human
who desires
to fuck a human
"sexed the same"
as he or she,
which stirs the,
to me,
more exhaustive question,
i.e.
is the comrade queer?

I mean,
does there lurk within
red comradeship's
ontology
some solvent
that the hierarchies
of "sex difference"
that make straightness
possible
just can't survive?

Is the comrade that queer form
which, while besieging
power's redoubts,
dismantles also
(useful comrade!)
those gendered identities
invented to divide and conquer,
in the happy

aftermath of which
no sex is straight?

Just some questions I propose for the next meeting of the Party
in Beijing, where functionaries concern-troll the modern use of
tóngzhì, which the kids made sodomitical. And if that Party wishes
to investigate a "socialism with v gay characteristics," then the
comrade's queerness isn't (only) awkward

but a nice occasion also
to infuse into the civic
song quotidian
the hope
that our desires
might lead us to
a supple sameness: reinvent
identity not as a cage
but as the unity in cumming,
quality of presence that
can feel like
dissolution into
a soft nothing
that's the whispered
hope inflecting every vision,
intimate
or world-historic,
of a paradisal clearing
where the flesh
can know at last
some pleasure,
a brief peace.

Dysphoria, Smoothed

In certain light you'd think the trail
of stubble left along my thighs
the first time I tried shaving them
could lead to a triangular
conjunction that some bigots say
means *woman*.

Woman means a life
I haven't lived, it's true,
but I was never all that keen
on such a stern word anyway.
Nor *man*! Just boi or girl
it's always been for me,
if what you want to do
is hail me.

Trimmed my pale bottom, too,
almost shaved it, but decided
I was not prepared
to risk an ingrown there,
unsightly ridge upon the smooth,
cathected-with-my-daydreams moon
I perch on, hiding hairs
by sitting languidly now,
in my briefs, before the desk
where I try harder than I should
to make you like me.

Yet there's just no reason
smooth should have to mean *untrue*. When I
let my glance condescend unto my thighs,
I see a femme surprise (!)
equivalent to what I feel,
have "always,"
in some fashion, felt
"inside me."

To match the outside to the in-,
however laboured or contrived
that process is? At bottom
it's just one more way
to help you find me.

portrait of the autist as a young whatever

what is this system of behaviour, I do not understand it and all my intuitions seem wrong

I shall study this!!

I have systematically theorized the norms and values of this system and will act in accordance with them, even at the expense of other norms and values I had previously theorized but am not currently obsessed with

~surprising amounts of success that also conceal devastating blind spots and imbalances and failure~

wait these norms I've "mastered" instrumentally are maybe actually intrinsically fucked???

wait I've misunderstood everything oh oh fuck

↓

"rebellion"/collapse

↓

recovery, recalibration

↓

repeat, perhaps with mitigation

↓

maybe begin to notice a pattern

↓

maybe begin to correct for it more adequately

↓

wonder if it's like this for everybody

↓

is it

riding

last night I had planned to go out to a party but then felt instead like just boarding the subway & riding & riding with my body quiet & deep in a book but it's hard to work up the resolve to do that so I went to the party & did what I could to contain all that riding inside me

warning

frequently adding "man" and "dude"
to the end of greetings,
men are so insistent
that you, too, be a man,
as if this makes it more certain
that they, too,
are men,

that all maleness's borders
are defended—

the way a flagging
imperial army
warns its fresh recruits
against desertion

anything you want

exhausted, I think:
I don't need to be trans,
I just want to be loved,
I'll be anything you want me to.

a thought that consistently
makes me feel trans as fuck.

transness as a condition of
I just want to be loved,
I'll be anything you want,
encountering
again and again
an internal limit.

the conclusions drawn
from that experience.
the steps taken.

Closet Exits Camouflaged

To be straight is to misconceive
how closets work. As if you just
malinger in a darkened chamber,
clarities
wrapped round your skin
like leopard print, self-knowledge
self-available, your only real
deficiency the courage to—
deep breath!—release the door
and step on out.

                    It's much weirder than that.

More often it's, insidiously,
a stiff, desperate fixity
of vision, earnest gaze unswerving
from one clear, respectable direction.
And/or just a No—
a vexed negation of a truth
that gives itself away by its
insistence. *No no no I'm not,*
I'm really not. Who said you were?
Which isn't to imply that all confessions
mean their opposites, but just to say
that closets operate this way
sometimes: a knowing that insinuates
itself beneath persuasive strata
of unknowing, where the captive in the dark
is there by choice and also not,
and definitely not the one
who shrouded the way out:

is not the faceless patriarch
who stands outside the closet door
and makes a noise that imitates
the cinching of a heavy lock.

"tough but fair"

child abuse language is domestic abuse language is cop language is
dad language is I'm warning you language is don't make me tell you
again is punishment language is the prison guard's language and we
learn it early is the torturer's language don't say I didn't warn you is
the seed of fascism already here

Spilling Over

Trotsky was born *Bronstein*! And you know
who else was: Samuel, Seagram's magnate, czar
of Judaic philanthropy in Canada—no, fuck,
that's *Bronfman*. I get Jews confused,

am Jewish so allowed to, though the funds
that nourished me in childhood and not only
then were, well, *suburban*: debt-inflected,
aspirant. Such high achievers, cocksure,

in my vastly Jewish high school class, a flexible
exceptionalism, evoking ghosts of fascist smears: both
bankers backing bosses *and* the labour leaders organizing
scrappy workers on the factory floor, we Jews, more

two-faced than a trick watch, we play every side,
suggested Adolf Hitler, a proud boy
and shitty painter from an empire that was Austria,
or? I get fascists confused, what with

the will to power in all of us (more honed in some).
In second grade the small Lev Bronstein
(that was Trotsky) organized his comrades
in short pants to rise against a teacher

who oppressed them. Vast Judeo-Bolshevik
conspiracies rode wild from France to Minsk
and further, if you believe Goebbels,
cut-rate ad man for Mercedes-Benz,

maker of fine automobiles lots of Jews
now drive, obeying road signs. You're no brother
of mine, I think as I read the latest online
cruelties, scared they might befall me, choose me.

Violence: oft-random. Be its agent
all your life and meet an ice pick, be mildness
personified and get killed just the same. Disaster.
Desolate, I read the rolls of my country's big bourgeoisie

in *Forbes*-adjacent, self-satiric magazines
and count the digits (ten!) in fortunes noted there,
and scan the names for *yiddishkeit*, and find it.
I find it also in lists of the great Red dead.

In Dublin once a boy who'd lived
his whole life in left movements said
to me I looked to him like a young Trotsky.
Took it, of course, as compliment,

and even now I feel a surge
of gender-blurring vanity
when it comes back to mind. It was a quip,
but in that callow moment I believed

in transformation. Got to know
another comrade *they*
I met there: wise and kind,
uncircumcised,

which seemed to me a mystery,
enigma bottomless. (Their firm
round bum right there.) I closed
my eyes. They kissed me like

romantic leads in spy films
from the 1940s liked to do,
anointing me the ingenue.
They were so broke,

kept running out
of credit on their phone, but hoped
to stay in touch, and so did I,
desire's an internationalism,

but anyway the poem turns gay
because I'm trying
somehow to say
I guess I've taken
the long, hard way back
to what I knew
at like sixteen,
which had to do
with freedom
as a spilling over
from one bright,
unbearable
impossibility
into the next,
a jailbreak
from nations
and histories
and plans,
the joy
winding arms
round the pain
that rips us to shreds,
unsurvivable
but without which
we're nothing already,
just gone,
irreparably forever
dispossessed

burrow

morning's a small dog I coax
from my warm bed, and when your scent
remains within my sheets I want
to keep that pup at bay until
the seas concede to the red blooms
of algae murdering sea life,
accelerating the sixth mass
extinction to have swept the planet
since it first was sullied by desires
we might call creaturely, I call

you, you don't answer,
blow me off next time I text,
my cock (if that's the name
that I'm now calling it) inside
your mouth was like
yours in my hand, I couldn't
tell the difference, I would like

to write a poem that offers what
pornography, I mean
porn at its best, can make
me feel, just good,
escape that maybe
names but doesn't
attempt to recuperate
how unjust power produces
what I want to come to,
what I don't. a small dog

wouldn't whimper half as much
as I do when I feel how capsized
I am before single bodies'
beauty, even when
I know collective beauty's more
reliable, more ethical
and needful now. if, watching seas'
disease proceed, I call
the dog back to my bed
and tuck us in, might we
be suffered to just slumber
for a while longer,
just a while, just for a little
moment longer

containment

you want to
contain the mistakes want to
say that then was the time I was making
mistakes but now I'm good I'm fine don't
mention the mistakes that preceded
that time (not even to yourself) don't
admit the possibility that you've
been wrong forever since
that might mean you're still
wrong now

Unseen

The women who raised me but were not my kin,
who walked from the bus to the house in all weather,
who had kids my age in Manila, and partners,
who sent money home to those loved ones, unseen
for a decade—
                    as, meanwhile, this house, stolen country
were so far from *mine* that the cries of those who'd
been here first, are here still, were as audible (after
you'd learned how to hear) as the train that would break
the pale silence at midnight in my childhood bedroom
where I would pretend to be sleeping, imagine
that I'd raised myself, that the loneliness of
kids my age in Manila had nothing to do
with the way that the halls of the house I grew up in
looked clean.

wager

whether to be hostile or hospitable
to the potentially murderous,
potentially life-giving
stranger
is the wager
at the root of most (all?)
politics

I mean, the political
seems constituted largely by
concentrically expanding
waves of wagers
re: how much or when
the stranger
can be trusted

probably love also
pivots on this wager, if
just in the moments after
and before it becomes love, I mean
the moments when love hasn't
yet become or is no longer
sovereign, when it hasn't yet
achieved or had achieved but lost
escape velocity
from the political

this situation vis-à-vis
the stranger means
compulsory risk

Rothko/Lupron

What goes together,
what doesn't: the parole officer's
makeup, immaculate; a pair
of replicated Rothkos
on the boardroom wall;
fluorescents and the man
who can't be named.

A drug called Lupron is what's offered
to such men, whose sex
harmed others. "Offered"
is violent misnomer: force,
or Faustian choice, imposes
chemical castration
on these men.

Prevention,
retribution:
hard to say
which motive is
most active.

And I wonder if
that forcibly dosed state would alter
how beauty struck the senses:
say, *disinterested*
enjoyment of the fine effect
of the official's labour
on herself, those unpaid hours;
the Rothkos on the wall, now thunderous
in their brute colouration, not just
patently absurd attempts
to civilize cold chambers
of state sanction. A rich meditation
for one not obliged
to live it.

Insistent, this urge I feel
to clarify how I was there
as volunteer, as visitor. To say
I'm not a criminal, but also
that I'm not the one so violated.
If I limp my dick it's my own choice.
My words, my clit, my gaze
remain a citizen's.

The man whose shadow falls over this poem
is more than six feet tall, is bulky, broad,
slow-moving. Throughout the poem
his confidentiality is kept.
You may have even passed him in the street.

civility

they'll evict you
in your own language,
they'll gender you correctly
as they cage you,
they'll look resigned
as they infiltrate and bomb you,
will say it's for your own good,
for the sake of your own freedom.
liberalism is a polite knife.

float

to choose vulnerability
as if it's a source
of pleasure, strength. but to choose it
even when life imposes it on you
at other times as diktat, as power:
the cop, the boss, the bully, the drone,
the landlord, the mistaken cell
repeating, the mistaken choice repeating,
the impossibility of knowing
what you don't yet know but need to.

to choose it, to choose
vulnerability anyway.
not as a wishing-away of power,
a spell for staying small,
but as the name for the empty,
habitable space
within the helix
of longing and aversion:
in the gravity of both,
but touching neither.

June to August

the fear says: by the time we
reach June we forget
ourselves again. as if the seasons'
changing could not only throw
your hormones into disarray but
also cause amnesia more
pervasive, might unknow you—
might cast what seems on happy days
like *growth* as just a sepia reel
projected on a you-shaped
silhouette. the fear, it says:

by the time we reach summer
we let heat unmoor what time's
taught us we need, as if the seeds
you thought you'd sown with care
in winter were just all along
some C4 in seed form, laid in
to blow apart what peace you've
lately maybe come by, maybe
found a way to better
offer others. that same fear's

not paranoia if by August
June feels like regression to a
mean that lurked there all along,
if by July you're saying, "well,
I guess the patterns are set early
and if you're bound to repeat
them at least maybe you can learn
to shield yourself and others
from them better, and that's progress
of a kind, it isn't nothing." like,
if now that longing,

call it restlessness or something
else that doesn't rhapsodize it,
that wide mood that seems to
conquer you each summer
hurts you more than it
hurts others, well, that's
something, given
there was never any
version of this story
where you weren't
going to get hurt

faintly

self as Russian doll,
ancient iterations dwindling
to motes, concentric
nuclei, evading
the unassisted eye, though
sometimes, even after
a long, long while,
when the light's just right:
a trace. smudge of a whale
in a still sea. still
alive

A Sense of History

I think of femboys all day long.
Sometimes of chlamydia
(its prevalence). The revolution
has to wait.

The Trotsky biopic, I hear,
is mostly fucking. Hard
to grasp
how in a revolutionary

moment
some could feel at once
libidinously energized
and happy to repress the drive

to spank a twink until integral
solidarities were won.
Kerensky is a name I learned
today. My sense of history

is shallow. My start
was in a finished
basement, where my closest friend
and I passed hours

in play
charged with desires
we couldn't name.
He married young,

is a small business
owner, maybe
counter-revolutionary,
uninvited to the Future,

and not just
because he'd make me blush.
Without so much as a complicit
flush of guilt or shame, we each

accepted what we felt
and even praised each other
for it, our shared, private
singularity.

The subject is divided, says Lacan, whom I can't read.
It's unclear whether we would even know if we were free.

Place

I have been here a while, and now might go.
Have found here what I wanted. Also failed to.
What power I have is gifted (stolen) from the earth,
or granted to me by comrades, with whom
I try to share it. I have been here
but now could leave, and go where I'm
not known—where maybe I could think
more clearly, be preoccupied by fewer ghosts.
What would I think of then? Or write about?
For whose sake would I struggle there? To whom
would I report? Freedom of that kind is boring,
maybe. Melancholy. Where I go, maybe
I'll find myself (the one I left behind, I mean,
much older now); I'll ask myself
with what I have been occupied out there
while I've been here, changing my name
but staying in place, bounded in lanes,
this garret-city, siloed space, this citadel
a short walk from the spot where I first breathed.
I know this place too well. I worry I
know this place far too well to ever leave.

prima donna

my rage is a diva orchid:
I neglect it
for just one second
and it wilts into despair

Where Tear Gas Can't Reach

I throw nuts at the cops from the cheap seats.
I'm so afraid of life. I hardly show it.
As a result I fear I'm not much use.
I throw nuts at the cops, *figuratively*.

Figuratively I have opinions, sometimes.
Or maybe just stand passive,
barefoot, in the river of what's possible
to think. The cops lick at my nuts.

I make them bitter. Try to vex the murderers.
It isn't much, but I try to make myself useful.
Civilizations honour courage. But when, uncivil,
you and I parade across the lawns of rich adjacencies

to power that are housed near the cave I touch myself
and sometimes you in, I can't bring myself to fling
a single thrill of excrement (even a dog's!)
at terrace windows. Class mobility is fake,

it's true. Though there are personalities to whom it seems
power just accrues, and, maybe, in the longer run,
those transformations that will make
class not a thing, abolition as renewal

of what's possible to think. But for now: so much violence.
I'm seldom brave enough to challenge it head-on.
I'm frank with you about this. You seem honestly
to love me anyway (it's nice that love can work like this,

though I suspect that desire can't, or doesn't often).
Sing as if to compensate: boldly, keen to translate rage
out of my body into sage contiguities with struggle
but located where tear gas can't reach.

I cocoon in pale speech. It won't be pardoned.

Visible to Vanishing

Sometimes I wish that my desire
for visibility would last
beyond a day or two before
it's swapped out for a dull wish
just to disappear. Slow drip of fear
that we whose bodies clamour after
transformation, hoping we
might match what the world sees
to what we feel, are moved most basically
by a despair of ever holding
power enough to make a change
in worlds beyond our bodies.

        But the paradox: from that despairing
        wish about the single body
        blooms a need to change those worlds
        as well, to make them safe enough
        and fertile of our pleasure, joy—wins
        that would be shared
        with every body. Futures where to swing
        from visible to vanishing
        could be a kind of play,

not an exhausting bipolarity
that makes some days impossible
to give account of, other days abundant, all
a next-to-hopeless seeking after
some new self who could amend
the world with voice, or, if not,
be so gentle, almost harmless in it.

"As for measure and other technical
apparatus, that's just common sense:
if you're going to buy a pair of pants
you want them to be tight enough so
everyone will want to go to bed with
you. There's nothing metaphysical
about it. Unless, of course, you flatter
yourself into thinking that what you're
experiencing is 'yearning.'"
—Frank O'Hara

Tight Pants

Entranced
pedestrians, in search
of flirty openings, ask me
the time. What
time does it
feel like to you?
It's probably that.
Still early, I step out,
with my coat's cut
enhancing gender mystery
so behind me
you can't tell
what my tight pants are hiding.
Don't mean to be furtive, but
the silver lining when you see
how badly you've misread me
is: how often does your dailiness
elicit true surprise?

Surmise: the yearning
I felt when
I met these pants
upon the rack
along which they
were agonized
is relative, proportionate
to yearnings
that I hope they conjure
in cute passersby.

This talk of *yearning*
needn't be
mere metaphysic.

Denim, bottom—these
materialities are thick
enough to dream on,
personalities themselves.
Don't stare but please do look.
That way I'll know I'm there.

either/or

writing (making) is hard, but not writing (not making) is sad. it follows that life is always either hard but not sad, sad but not hard, or both hard and sad. perhaps most commonly, life is sad then hard then sad in a flutter-quick alternation that feels like, but is not, simultaneity. there can be no period of time during which life is neither hard nor sad, because one is always either writing (making) or not writing (not making). rude

Spectacle

Like the most moving credit card ads you've ever seen, neoliberalism and fascism both stage epics of triumphant agency atop hidden, sedimented, violent structure. Their great promise is voice. *You*, they say. *Now you'll be heard.*

What they don't say, but mean: *We'll give you voice, but no exit. Agency, but only where you assent to structure. We'll project your silhouette on a magic lantern screen so you'll appear to certain others like a giant, heroic, vast continents of you, and this we'll call deliverance from humiliation, even dignity, but we won't succour that projected body you live in, which must remain unhappy, frail, rent with unmanageable want*—crushed in the end by structure. Under neoliberalism, under fascism, the relation between agency and structure is so occulted that wherever you think you've emerged from the labyrinth and found an effective politics, a vestibule opening onto history, you step a step or two further and find night.

Such politics are cruel and sentimental and, in the literal sense, spectacular. To be a neoliberal is to generate the spectacle and disavow its character and function. To be a fascist is to generate it, become it, and adore it. The distinction exists but isn't stark.

Degenerate

Specimen: male, oversexed,
inflicts himself on world's landscape,
does damage as he tries to make
a generative principle
in him take shape outside himself.

So goes the standard narrative,
acceptable hypothesis,
oft-fundable, if fungible,
an alibi.

Repressed the counterfactual: such dicks
adventure *not* to make life grow,
to people all the world with bright new beings,
but instead to make it all disintegrate,
to usher in disaster, court it,
Hoffman in *The Graduate*,
chasing death right to the altar,
fact unalterable and wry: sometimes
we crave sex since it unbinds,
destroys.

From these data, we deduce
our specimen, that male, much sexed,
is driven by a need to smash
the stone the public 'graves him in,
to unravel himself until
it's so unclear where his humiliation stops
and his rictus of bliss begins
that clinical observers can
but pity him, and wonder.

Transparencies

An openness performed, sometimes,
abets you to conceal a closure
from yourself. For instance, I've
observed that people in a closet
sometimes punish you severely
for possessing enough hubris
to reveal them to themselves
in ways unwonted, if
extraordinarily wanted,
a pun that confuses people
when this poem is read out loud,
unwonted with an *o* being
archaic, rarely spoken by
we lucky ones begotten after
sex began in 1963, and we desublimated
all our fantasies (not all),
and claimed we were now free (lmao),
and said now we would say it all,
and said it all, and suffered.

Committed to transparency
re: intimacy, even re:
our regimented deviancy,
we're so clear (a clarity
that also can deceive) to everyone
except ourselves, and when
in spite of all our performed openness
we're seen, what's left to us
amounts to what the older
generations got: a trembling
in the gaze of beauty that disdains
to kill us for the moment, and
a nauseating, self-defeating rage.

innocence isn't the opposite of violence

they say it's the guilty who are violent
so earn prison, deserve suffering,
but in my experience? like, watching cops
inflict atrocities on those who cross them,
brawlers who see nothing
wrong with using "necessary force"
to guard themselves, "protect
the vulnerable," endlessly available
defence of self-defence, the sergeant's
vicious blow to the handcuffed
"guilty"—I mean, this is just to say

in my experience?
proud innocence

does as much grievous harm.

Crow

A man I'll never be as good as
has his goodness rhapsodized
deservedly before a crowd of crows.
The orator, his friend, a seal,
pronounces histories of kindness
that the decent man has sown, his legacy.

I don't mean that ironically,
though my respect's inflected
by the way I feel disqualified already
from encomia like that,
which would in my case be just flattery,
pretense. And still, in unrepairable
creatureliness I bark for praise,
spend days retracing the shores
of the slow dream the lake was
when I didn't feel so compromised,
the way a shimmering wedge of it
blued down beyond the domino metropolis,
the dense downtown it edged
to panting, as observed from narrow ledges,
the shit job I had then blued
by a hard boss who erotized
paternities that reputation, money
lent him over me, one cruel man in a line of many
I looked up to. I can't understand
(of course I can) just why I so identified
with all the fathers and Great Men,
those momentary victors
who had always made me
feel *less than*, if sometimes promising
(an answer) junior standing
in the bloodstained ink lines
they presided over. If I'd married

young like the man the tall room crowed for,
been humble enough to see
in family, work, community
a life containing most of what there is
to live for, maybe I could hope
to deserve words someday
like those the seal barked
eloquently for him. But

in creatureliness intractable
I swing instead
from branch
to fragile branch

doing what you're supposed to

kind of just like a dog
who keeps transiting
terrified squirrels
to her mortified human
& smiling & snuffling with joy
as she thinks she's fulfilling
her good good essence, is completing
her most basic task
as she must
if she hopes
to be loved

rehearsal

why can't my selfies do my writing for me?
like, after all, they claim to be my "self"?
I take so many, I could make a chapbook:
every nude a sonnet, bum as volta.

it was, in fact, around the time my selfie-
taking ramped up that I started writing poems
again. (discuss.) and these poems were effectively
word-selfies, though they had a kind of...idk...
futurity (?) the photos lacked. more telegraph
sent from a few months down the road than
photograph of now, they rehearsed possibilities
for what my body and desire might curl
towards, extend into, if I could sort out how.

self-portraiture as wish, as howl for love
that says love me *this* way, not as I was. as *this*.

lines

the one-bedroom apartment
priced out of reach
of grocery cashiers
is a front line.

and the wake of a fishing boat
hauling lobsters in defiance
of white settlers' rage
is a front line, and the burnt tires
at a construction site
on stolen land,
and the warehouse floor,
the app courier's full bladder
and no open toilet,
the teachers' staff room table
piled with masks inadequate
to block a plague,
the maps that elide
where the state has no title,
where it squats, soiling rivers,
surveilling healing lodges
built in dignified defiance—
lines upon lines.

front after front
and another front opens.
to sit in a room and write lines
that are merely descriptive
feels barren. prescription,
presumptuous. the mode of these lines
is then *wish*:
breath urging the wind to lift lines
where the struggle unfolds
into prismatic genome,
arcane origami,
its vertices rising
into something shaped like a horse
large enough to hold
armies of wronged:

undefeated despair
become force.

for Chile, on the day after a status-quo federal election in the Canadian state

"they stole so much from us they even
stole our fear."

most daily papers hardly note
how the protests spread from schoolkids
leaping transit gates to union comrades
downing tools. *disorder*'s what
the techno-barons' outlets say.
a monstrous mass, belligerent:
austerities that animate it
(stole so much from us they even—), the build
to the breaking point erased. tanks in the streets
make elders think of Pinochet. the young
where I live see, online, those schoolkids
who look just like them
enacting a defiance that's so simple,
so impossible: *you can do that?*
just leap over the barricades?
refuse to pay?
reject outright
their terms of play?
together?

movement

if organizers in Hong Kong share tactics
with their peers in Santiago, who then whisper
thru WhatsApp to friends in Quito, who have tips
that Lebanese trade-unionists can make
incendiary use of;

and if that love affair you had
(which changed what you imagined
could be possible) years earlier
with a comrade
in another country
is stirred once more,
ghostly, in your body
by the sense you're now in struggle
in the selfsame way that lover
across fictive borders is;

and if when teachers strike the flight
attendants strike; the word gets out
this works; the cops come out in force
because the threat of working people's
solidarity is real, the struggle backed
by those who can no longer work
or never could, the riot and the strike
in striking, riotous harmony, the struggle led
not by the old industrial class alone
but also by those the factory needs and hides:
healers of bodies, forgers of minds,
who walk the picket line and then
go home to prepare lunches
for the kids dependent
on school programs
for a meal;

if word of such devices spreads,
and more than word,
it may not be just capital that overcomes
the hardened borders of the future
capital's intent that most of us won't see.
it may not be just influence, hegemony.
it may be us, and those of us
we haven't yet begun
to think about as *us*,
who move.

manifest

the French for *protest* seems to me
a better name than *demonstration.*
manifestation is right: to manifest,
make manifest a fact unseen
but felt intensely, and by many. like:
the clamorous hundred thousands
who thronged Québec's streets
throughout the Maple Spring—
the hidden currents
those rare days made plain.

and when we now reclaim the streets
in Anglo citadels of shame
where presbyters' commercial mores
distort the rents beyond affording—
what seams of desire does this illuminate?

what would it take to seize the need
for meaning lived collectively
and fill it out with substance that
eventually would demand
to be manifest en masse—in shoreless
crowds whose selfies meant self-hope,
and not the poisonous despair
of feeling so much want and vision
trapped in your skin's borders,
with no means
to get it out, to give it form?

to manufacture from it
festivals

a simile is more honest than a metaphor thank you no questions at this time

I have an (actually) autistic relationship to metaphor, which is to say
I have trouble with the slippages involved in claiming two things
are the same when clearly they're not, and you might ask
(I wouldn't, but you might) what kind of poetry can do without
metaphor, can resist saying a rent strike is a rising tide
or a riot is a harvest moon, is this not an impoverishment etc.,
is this not a falling away from the heights to which language
aspires? maybe, but my brain never tires of going like:
suffering isn't bravery those are different things let someone say it.
to absorb an injustice when you have no choice isn't courage
don't let them say that. a habit isn't a need unless
it is. a friend isn't a comrade unless they are.
a comrade isn't salvation, but enough of us
struggling together may be. this scream
is a song. no it isn't. it is.

NOTES AND ACKNOWLEDGEMENTS

Works and workers cited, or otherwise present, in something like chronological order:

Walter Benjamin and his notion of "messianic time," as it appears in his essay "On the Concept of History"; the #TakeBackTPL protest, and everyone who organized and attended it; Zoe Whittall, who did a really moving tweet about it; Sean Bonney (especially his poem "ACAB: A Nursery Rhyme") and everyone else who finds novel ways to say fuck the police; *The Coming Insurrection* by The Invisible Committee; everyone who said abolish means abolish in the summer of 2020, building on a foundation laid by Black abolitionists like Mariame Kaba, Angela Davis, and Ruth Wilson Gilmore, who have been saying it so eloquently for so long; Marx and Engels's good post, "The philosophers have only interpreted the world, in various ways; the point, however, is to change it," and their other solid post, "Communism is for us not a *state of affairs* which is to be established, an *ideal* to which reality [will] have to adjust itself. We call communism the *real* movement which abolishes the present state of things. The conditions of this movement result from the premises now in existence"; Miguel James's poem "Against the Police"; Anne Boyer's poem "No"; Harry Josephine Giles's poem sequence *Abolish the Police*; a poem I've never read by A. Light Zachary, because trans consciousness is fractal and inscrutably collective; Jodi Dean's lecture "Four Theses on the Comrade," drawing on the work of Hongwei Bao; equally, the vision of the comrade in Wendy Trevino's poem "Revolutionary Letter"; autistic people, who help each other understand our experiences (and help each other adapt, build community, transform) with much more precision and care than regimes of medicalization governed by non-autistic people; Aida Sagadraca, Rosie Caledon, Gina and Francis Pineda-Jose, and everyone else who performs invisibilized, undervalued care work; the members and organizations of the Ontario Mennonite community dedicated to restorative justice, and the prisoners and former prisoners who testify to that work's value as well as its limits; Kai Cheng Thom's pathbreaking writings on love, sex, gender, justice, and community, some of them collected in the book *I Hope We Choose Love: A Trans Girl's Notes from the End of the World*; Mercedes Eng's *Prison Industrial Complex Explodes*; Frank O'Hara's feelings about pants, Albert O. Hirschman's exit vs. voice distinction, Leo Bersani's essay "Is the Rectum a Grave?", Philip Larkin's poem "Annus Mirabilis," Herman Marcuse's notion of repressive desublimation, and Rainer Maria Rilke's first Duino Elegy; the Mi'kmaw fishers resisting settler violence, the Six Nations land defenders at 1492 Land Back Lane, the Wet'suwet'en people defending their territory from colonial invasion, and all the tenants and workers organizing themselves in and against dire conditions during the pandemic and before it; John Berger and his term "undefeated despair," which he used to describe Palestinian resistance to the Israeli state's military occupation; Jérôme Duval, "Chili: « Ils nous ont tant volé, qu'ils nous ont même pris notre peur »," *Politis*, October 22, 2019; Joshua Clover on riots and strikes; the Fight for $15 and Fairness movement (now called Justice for Workers) and the Workers' Action Centre in Toronto, under the leadership of Deena Ladd and Pam Frache, among others, which taught me what broad-based social movement organizing could look like; Sue Ferguson, who introduced me to social reproduction theory; the Toronto New Socialists and the New Socialist Group—especially Todd Gordon, who invited me into that network and gave me a political home where I could unpack my experiences in social movements; comrades in Artists for Climate & Migrant Justice and Indigenous Sovereignty (ACMJIS), who created a useful space for collective questioning of the liberal political imagination that permeates so many arts institutions in so-called Canada; and *We Want It All: An Anthology of Radical Trans Poetics*, co-edited by Andrea Abi-Karam and Kay Gabriel, which affirms an intuition that animates *Plenitude*, too: that revolutionary socialist politics, trans experience, and poetry can be generative in each other's company, and it's cool and good when they meet.

Thanks to the editors of the following publications, where some of *Plenitude*'s poems first appeared, usually in earlier versions:
· *Briarpatch Magazine* ("a simile is more honest than a metaphor thank you no questions at this time"; "movement")
· *Grain Magazine* ("doing what you're supposed to")
· *The Malahat Review* ("Against the Law"; "hustle")
· *Plenitude Magazine* ("Closet Exits Camouflaged")
· *PRISM international* ("Tight Pants")
· *Protean Magazine* ("energy")
· *The Puritan* ("burrow"; "Plenitude")
The poem "June to August" was written for and first presented at the Probably Poetry reading series in Toronto; thanks to its organizers.

Lots of gratitude for the support of the Canada Council for the Arts and of the Ontario Arts Council through its Recommender Grants for Writers program. Thanks to my agent Stephanie Sinclair for heartening enthusiasm and thoughtful, steadfast advocacy. And to Jay, Hazel, and the whole team at Book*hug for believing in this project and working with care and dedication on its behalf (and recommending it for that OAC grant). Thanks to kin and friends and loves and comrades, especially Kirah, Hayleigh, and Ariana, who listened to and shared encouragement about rough drafts of *Plenitude*'s poems. Thanks to my parents Roz and Lorne, and to my sibling Adam. Special thanks to Mirka for limitless honks, among other things. And to A. Light Zachary for sweating every comma alongside me, with patience, precision, and grace.

ABOUT THE AUTHOR

Photo: Daniel Sarah Karasik

Daniel Sarah Karasik (they/them) is the author of five previous books, including the poetry collection *Hungry* and the short story collection *Faithful and Other Stories*. Their work has been recognized with the Toronto Arts Foundation's Emerging Artist Award, the CBC Short Story Prize, and the Canadian Jewish Playwriting Award. They organize with the network Artists for Climate & Migrant Justice and Indigenous Sovereignty (ACMJIS), among other groups, and are the founding managing editor of *Midnight Sun*, a magazine of socialist strategy, analysis, and culture. They live in Toronto.

Colophon

Manufactured as the first edition of
Plenitude
in the spring of 2022 by Book*hug Press

Edited for the press by A. Light Zachary
Copy edited by Andrea Waters
Proofread by Rachel Gerry
Cover background image: istock.com/kely
Typesetting + design by Lind Design
Type: Kievit Serif and Neue Plak

Printed in Canada

bookhugpress.ca